The Four Queens

Understanding the Powers of the Crown

The Four Queens

ISBN-13 978-1503045248

ISBN- 10:1503045242

Library of Congress Cataloging –in-Publication Data

Printed in United States of America

DEDICATION

Peace and Blessings! This book is dedicated to my three "SUNS," Terrence (RIP), Devin, and Rushion. Always know that you can achieve your goals, regardless of the adversities that you may face in life. My GrandStars Kari and Arrionna, I'm building a legacy for you. To my beautiful mother (Margaret Clark), Queen, as I always tell you, words are too simple to express my love for you. Simply put, you are our everything. To my brothers Shawn and Henry, thanks for your undying love and support. To my sisters Yoshida, Tosha and Quesha, I love you more than you'll ever know. Pops (Greg Gibson), I learned a lot from you; wish I would've listened more (RIP). To my Grand Parents, Louise Clark, Thomas and Mary Gibson (RIP), thanks for always loving and being there for me, you'll always be remembered.

REVIEWS

Alex Clark is an old soul. Like a wise cartographer he maps a beautiful tapestry of wisdom regarding women. Playing off the symbolic meaning of the queen cards in the deck he introduces us to different typologies of womanhood. There is a serious playfulness he employs by showing how what we may consider a vice of each Queen reveals a deeper virtuous energy. What we find in this timely, practical and engaging text is a powerful spiritual affirmation of womanhood.

Anthony Smith, Author and Community Activist

The Four Queens: Understanding the Powers of the Crown by Alex Clark is a book that I would categorize as a self- help. It introduces four natures of women using the analogy of the Queens in a deck of cards.

Throughout the book the author also includes affirmations, quotes, and references that supports his perspective and further engages the reader. I truly enjoyed reading this book! It's a quick read packed with wisdom. The book is a great for both men and women. As the author concludes "Master them (Queens), and you master yourself...Put your crown on and wear it with dignity."

Tonya Miller-Cross, Entrepreneur and Community Activist

This book gives a riveting account of the awakening of a female's inner spirit. Alex Clark introduces women one by one to their possibilities. Grab a hold of this book and begin catching your Blessings. There is a new journey involving the Soul of the reader.

Mercedes Harrington, Author and Entrepreneur

Brilliant, flowing read that held me captive from the first sentence. Right away I identified with the four queens, and could name friends that could fit the description of each one, including myself. A highly-satisfying page turner, one that ladies of all ages will find pieces of themselves in. This will be the first of many great books form Alex Clark. I truly enjoyed this book!

Arnisha Archie

The Four Queens: Understanding the Powers of the Crown so profoundly, eloquently and tastefully written by Alex Clark paints a vivid depiction of the attributes, morals, and downfalls of women. I am amazed at how Alex took the four queens from a deck of playing cards and transformed them into the complete queen women should strive to become. Alex kept my attention from the beginning to the end, as he carefully wove and blended textures and fibers to create this amazing queen who's loving, ambitious, savvy, disciplined and graceful. The Four Queens inspired me to do a reassessment of the desires of my heart, become more in-tune with my spirit, live life to the fullest and become a better me. Because of *The Four Queens*, I understand the powers of my crown and I am well suited for any given day. This book is a must have for men and women.

Alisha N. Byrd, Author and Entrepreneur

Alex Clark

CONTENTS

ACKNOWLEDGMENTS

I would like to extend my Sincerest Gratitude to the beautiful Queens who dissected my every word. Trust me, I really appreciate all of the valuable insight and literary advice that you gave me. (The Queens) Ed Woods, Alisha Byrd, and Stephanie Polk; thanks for pushing me to get this project done. I must admit the dialogue was great. But, ya'll can be hard on a man (Margaret Clark, Ms. Phillips, Karen Brown, Joyce Bailey, Monica Morehead-McKenzie, Dr. Janelle Williams, Phoebe Gillespie, Linda Woods, Tiffini Simpson, Amanda Chalk, Aunt Brenda Chalk, Crystal Key, Ms. Brown, Linda Brooks, Shamil Connor, Candy Brown, Queen Mother Ama Bey, Carmen Horn, Tia Glass, Gylanda Graham, Cheryl Blackman, Montoya McCombs, Shawanna Godfrey, Tonya Miller-Cross, Arnisha Kitchen-Archie, Mercedes Harrington, and Mrs. Powell). To the Brothers who read this before it was a book, you can finally get a copy Greg Butler, Eric Martin-El, C-Lo Redman, Gene Wade, Nico Sanders, Andre Clodfelter, Corey Alexander, Rod, Born, The A-Alikes, Garry Robinson, Dwon Chalk, Napoleon Goodson (Polo), Sean Ingram, Reginald Usury, Antonio Randolph, Leroy "Skip" Jackson, William Carrol, Omekas Moaney, Arron Battle, Jermaine Pierre Thomas, Salaam, Lee Brags, and anyone that I forgot. Special thanks to Pierre, Gary Hilliard, Marlon Connor and Mitchell Smith. Eddie Smith, thanks for your assistance with the cover.

Preface

Believe it or not, this book derived from a conversation between two friends (Steven "Quick" Johnson and I) having an in-depth conversation about women while playing a game of cards. Being that each suit represents a different strength or quality, I forgot about the game and started thinking about the symbolism of each suit and how I could make them relevant to TRYING to figure out one of the world's greatest, mysteries. Are you ready for this? WOMEN. Yes, WOMEN! The most mind boggling creation on the face of the earth.

This book is an attempt to give what I consider insight to the different personalities of women based on my knowledge and observation of them over the course of my life. I strongly believe that every woman possesses many of the traits and characteristics of each of the Queens presented here. Of course, some traits are more dominant and prevalent than others and—of course—every woman has a special and unique quality about herself; however, it is my hope that an understanding of what I have written about each of the queens will render a greater appreciation for women everywhere.

First, and foremost, this book is for the empowerment of women, as well as for the much-needed edification of men, who are sometimes totally oblivious to the spiritual, mental, emotional, and physical make-up of the women they are surrounded by every day.

This book should be read with an open-mind before an opinion can be *truly voiced, because certainly some of the principles and scenarios have not been experienced personally by some of the women who will read it; however, the principles and scenarios presented are to instill in women the desire to totally embrace everything positive about herself—from the outer physical appearance, to the inner soul and all that it governs; to the spirit which encourages one to partake of all the good that our Creator has provided; and everything in between that lends itself to taking the necessary measures to develop a nurturing, loving, positive self-image.*

Men who read this book please understand and see that each individual Queen's traits can actually be found collectively embodied in one woman. In other words, EVERY QUEEN IS EVERY WOMAN. The Queen of Hearts trait in a woman will love you. The Queen of Clubs in her will give you pleasure. The Queen of Diamonds in her will support you. But, the Queen of Spades in her can absolutely destroy you.

"Learning about love comes from within. It cannot be given. It cannot be taken away. It grows from your ability to re-create within yourself, the essence of loving experiences you have in your life"...

(Iyanla Vanzant)

1

THE QUEEN OF HEARTS

The Queen of Hearts is motivated by love and romance. She has a natural gift when it comes to the affairs of the heart, and she loves deep and strong. She personifies the spirit of love and femininity in its purest form. This Queen knows and fully understands the significance of fostering a loving and nurturing relationship with herself first, which allows her to share her love with others unselfishly. She believes in the Golden Rule with all of her heart and soul, and the Golden Rule is: "Treat others the way you want to be treated." She takes seriously that Love should never be taken for granted or abused; it should be cherished and protected by its possessor. It is her power to love that makes her so special and appealing beyond her physical features. Indeed, her weapon of choice is Love, because she knows when all else fails, Love conquers.

This Queen is very affectionate and thinks with her heart first. She believes being able to express her innermost feelings is an invaluable strength, as well as a mechanism to purge herself of the negativity that could impede her from being peaceful and loving. Her ability to perceive the needs of others before they can ask, and assisting them without expecting anything in return is what distinguishes her from someone who extends themselves for personal gains and accolades.

She sees the good in people before their character flaws can register in her mind. She doesn't judge people based on their physical appearance alone, because she understands that we as individuals are attracted to different types of beauty. She has learned to appreciate the uniqueness in everyone she meets, and she encourages them to embrace their uniqueness and to love themselves in every way possible. The Queen of Hearts doesn't allow what the media's perception of beauty is to keep her from feeling beautiful. She knows that there is only one of her on the planet, and to allow someone else's standard of what's beautiful and sociably acceptable makes her feel less than the Queen she is, is totally beneath her.

Her aura radiates confidence, warmth, compassion, tenderness, and a quiet strength; and her skin has a natural hypnotic glow that is mesmerizing. You can actually feel her presence when she enters the room, due to the fact that her beautiful spirit vibrates at a higher frequency. She meditates and prays to stay at peace with herself and the Creator, and she firmly believes that a family that prays together stays together. Just seeing this woman reassures you that life is truly a blessing worth cherishing; regardless of your current station in life.

By nature, this Queen is a mother to the world, and she sincerely believes in the African Proverb: "It takes a village to raise a child." This Queen has been blessed with an extra dose of motherly love. She will literally go out of her way to make sure that a child is fed, clothed, and has a place to stay—even if it's at her house. Her ability to nurture and love a child back to good health is truly amazing, as if she has supernatural powers that only the Queen of Hearts possesses. Children feel safe and secure in her presence, and she also has the ability to make total strangers feel as if they have known her all of their lives. This woman is family oriented, and she will sacrifice all of her comforts for the well-being of her family, friends, and love ones.

This Queen's home is filled with an abundance of love, peace, happiness, and serenity. From the moment you enter it feels as if the weight of the world has been lifted off of your shoulders. You could've had the so-called worst day of your life; however, it's something about the ambiance of this Queen's home that makes your worries seem so insignificant. The environment is so peaceful, relaxing, and stress-free; accompanied by feel-good music, exotic flowers, abstract art, and statues of lovers in a passionate embrace. But, what makes her home different from many others is, her Divine presence and motherly love. Everything about this Queen's home reminds you of how love should feel and be. It's like being in the Garden of Eden with permission to feast on every tree in sight. Visiting this Queen's home is synonymous to going over your grandmother's house and getting nurtured and spoiled like only your grandmother can do. What a feeling!

This Queen is a helpless romantic and she wholeheartedly believes in the *power of love and its many promises with everything in her being. She loves to be pampered and catered to, and she takes pride in doing what is necessary to keep her temple (body) pure and filled with positive energy. Her philosophy is: "If you feel good about yourself, you will strive to be in harmony with the laws of Mother Nature with your every action." Being showered with gifts, flowers, candlelight dinners, quiet evenings, good conversation, walks in the park, being spontaneous, and all of the little things that other women may take for granted, makes life worth living for this loving, passionate, yet simple* woman. She loves romance novels, cries at movies, and often fantasizes about being swept off her feet by Prince Charming and living happily ever after, that is, if she is not already taken. This Queen knows that love is the lifeline of human existence, so to be blessed with someone who understands this undeniable fact fulfills her every need, wish, and desire in a soul-mate.

Being that she is so passionate about loving and being loved, she is definitely willing to go that extra mile for her significant other. When it comes to their relationship, she values their union above anything else.

Simply put, the relationship that she has with the Creator and her mate comes first. This woman commits with her whole being; spirit, mind, body, soul, heart, and resources. There is no such thing as giving half of her love; it's all or nothing with her, and she demands the same energy and effort in return. Her quest is to make her relationship a replica of heaven on earth.

This Queen is very comfortable with her sexuality, and with the right King she has an insatiable appetite for romance, intimacy, and pleasure. She knows and understands that the mind is the biggest sexual organ, for the mind is the first recipient of the appeal that leads to the stimulation of all of the other erogenous zones. She is highly skilled in the art of making love, not just to the body, but also to the spirit, soul, and mind. Whether knowingly or unknowingly, she exercises the art of love making much like those revealed in the ancient secrets of the Kama Sutra, Tantric Yoga, Erotica, Sensual Massages, Visual Ecstasy, and Special Aphrodisiacs that are sure to get her lover in the mood for what will be the ultimate, unforgettable experience. Making love is extremely sacred to her, and she does it with so much *passion and enthusiasm. When it's time to get intimate with her significant other, the goal is to bring all of both his and her wildest fantasies to life. She is definitely a lady in public—demur and refined. But when the lights go down behind closed doors, she morphs into a sex-goddess and her King's every wish becomes her command. Yet, she is still in control even when she is being submissive. And—for certain—she keeps a bag of tricks to make sure things stay spicy in the bedroom.*

The Queen of Hearts understands that love is symbolic to water because of its softness and ability to fit every mould. However, within the softness of water, there is a power that can make the hardest elements wither away in time. Love isn't just soft and mushy. Love is being able to give, to endure, to empathize, to be just and firm, but most importantly, Love is the most powerful force in the universe. As long as this Queen stays in tune with her divine nature, she will wear her Crown with honor, pride, and integrity.

DOWNFALL

If the Queen of Hearts allows her kindness to be taken for a weakness, she will be a constant target for those who profit from playing games with the minds and emotions of the kindhearted. Because she thinks with her heart first, she often overlooks the obvious signs and red-flags, which can be extremely detrimental to her life, her health, and her well-being. Unfortunately, by thinking with her heart first, she is often blinded by the harsh reality that everyone she knows or meets doesn't have her best interest in mind. Although she has an idealistic view of how the world should be, she fails to realize that everyone doesn't see the world through her loving eyes.

If she didn't have her father in her life as a child or a strong male presence to demonstrate how a woman should be treated, she often looks for love, affection, and attention in the wrongs places. As a result, her longing to be loved and respected often causes her to use her body to get the attention and love that she desperately desires. Unfortunately, if she allows herself to be treated like an object—opposed to the beautiful Queen she is—this treatment will more than likely lead to unfulfilled relationships with men who don't have any intentions of getting to know who she is beyond her body.

Eventually, too much heartbreak from being so loving, nurturing, and trusting, will turn her sweetness into bitterness or, at the worse, acid. In this state, a loving, caring woman becomes vindictive and sexually reckless, and proves that no one can manipulate another person's emotions like the Queen of Hearts.

Although she is the Queen of Hearts, even for her, it is impossible to be everything to everyone. However, when it gets to the point where she stops loving and starts hating because she has been dethroned even after giving her all, she becomes the personification of the saying, "It's a thin line between love and hate," and there is NOTHING like the wrath of a woman who has been betrayed, humiliated and scorned.

Queen of Hearts, always remember to love yourself first and you will attract that special someone who will freely give you the love, honor, and respect you truly deserve. It is extremely important to understand that a man cannot complete you, he can only complement you. You are not an object, a punching bag, and you should never settle for any type of abuse.

It has been said that love conquers all, and it definitely takes a spiritually strong, loving, selfless, and dedicated woman to do the things you have been destined to do in a world full filled with hatred and despair. Your presence alone possesses the power to restore harmony, balance and order in the most chaotic situations. It is so true that a woman's job is never done; however, with a heart filled with love and sincere intentions, you will move mountains as if they were as light as the feather of Maat.

A wise man once said that a nation can rise no higher than its Woman, and when this profound, indisputable truth, is fully embraced and properly understood the world will become a much better place because of women like yourself.

After all, you are a mother to the world by nature. So, please keep loving, nurturing, healing, supporting, empowering, enriching our lives of others, and demonstrating how to be better people through the majestic power of love.

KEEP ON LOVING QUEEN

AFFIRMATION

OF THE QUEEN OF HEARTS

I Am, the embodiment of Queen of Hearts. I Am, the feminine expression of the Creator. It is through me that love comes into the world. I will embrace my divinity and love myself completely.

I AM the Queen of Hearts!

"*Who knows what tomorrow may bring; or when this adventure filled journey called life will be over? No one but the Creator...So today is perfect for enjoying the many wonders that life has graciously shared with us*"...

Maa-Kheru

2

THE QUEEN OF CLUBS

The Queen of Clubs is motivated by pleasure-seeking and socializing. She has a natural gift when it comes to organizing and bringing people together to have an unforgettable time. This Queen knows and fully understands the significance of experiencing the many facets of life, and has a pleasurable time while you doing it. She also believes in the Golden Rule with all of her heart and soul, and the Golden Rule is: "You're not promised tomorrow, so enjoy yourself to the absolute fullest while you're still living, because life is too short for any regrets." Her motto is to never miss out on an opportunity to mix and mingle, and spread some positive energy with the people you love. This Queen believes every day is a reason to enjoy life and have a party, and if you're around this woman long enough, you will find yourself dancing to the rhythm of her drum.

This Queen is very outgoing and free-spirited, and she refuses to allow the stress and strife that we are sometimes forced to endure impede her from experiencing the happiness that feeds her soul. She takes pride in her unique ability to view the world through the lens of a kaleidoscope and brings the many pieces and elements of this beautiful puzzle called life together to create unforgettable memories.

She has been blessed with the gift to unify people from all walks of life, cultures and ethnicities—bringing them together for one common cause. Of course that cause is to put your troubles on a shelf so you can "get ya groove on" and Turn Up!

Being that she is a true socialite, she is the person who frequents all of the hot-spots and knows who's from the most influential to the lowest of the low. Her friends and associates are from all walks of life and various professions, and they know how to get the party started. She is well connected on the club scene, so if you are looking for the hottest spots and events in town, she is definitely the Queen to consult. Her digits should definitely be on speed dial. This Queen can accommodate you and your guest, regardless of your social and financial status. She knows people from all walks of life love and enjoys the company of others in an environment that is filled with laughter and excitement.

Anything is subject to happen at a party or social gathering, and her objective is to capitalize on the many opportunities that may be present. Her thought process is linear because her primary focus is based on how she can make others feel good by socializing and dancing their troubles away.

This Queen is a club owner's dream. When she arrives on a scene, she is never alone; she brings the

party to the club. And of course,
there will be a substantial increase of
beverages sold at the bar. Her mind
is set on having a great time, making
new friends, networking, and possibly
meeting someone special. This Queen's
name headlines the V.I.P List. People
are naturally attracted to her
magnetic personality, and being in
her presence causes energy levels to
rise, and men literally fawn to buy
rounds of drinks with hopes of being
one of the lucky guys to enjoy her
much sought after company.

This Queen doesn't discriminate
when it comes to getting her groove
on. Her main objective is to have fun

and dance the night away. In other words, from classy to hole-in-the-wall, she is there for one reason—TO PARTY-- and to keep things real, she will add with much quickness, "And ain't nothing wrong with a liquor house party either." She is a walking billboard that reads: I KNOW WHERE THE PARTY'S AT!

Naturally, this Queen is an excellent dancer. When she takes the floor all eyes are glued to her body like an action packed movie. She uses her body like an instrument she's spent years mastering. She turns the dance floor into her private sanctuary. Every movement, every *dip, twist, turn and step are executed perfectly in harmony with the rhythm of the music. Whether she dances on beat, off beat, or in and out of the beat, she is the master the beat; yet, she becomes a slave to the rhythm of the beat, and is so possessed by it that she can lead the latest line dance, glide doing the Electric Slide, seductively roll her hips as she Cha-Cha, or playfully sway back and forth to old school jams. Depending on the event, her repertoire also includes the Viennese Waltz and The Tango. But no matter the genre, she rules the floor. Dancing is also how she relieves stress and centers her being, for it is* the sacred language known as BODY TALK, which she interprets and speaks fluently.

This Queen is articulate and possesses the social skills to mix and mingle with people regardless of their social status. Whether it be a diplomat, politician, lawyer, business tycoon, hustler, thug, or the average Joe, she puts everyone at ease and converses with them in the most attentive manner. Her networking and communication skills are also what makes her a valuable asset to her friends and associates. Being constantly on the scene, she is more inclined to know who's doing what, as well as how to get in touch with major movers and shakers. Although she loves a good party, she is also about handling her business. After all, she is The Queen of Clubs.

Regardless of the occasion, she displays her versatility like the true socialite she is by nature. If duty calls for some heels and a skirt, expect her to dress sexy but tasteful. If she's invited to a charitable event, such as a fundraiser or the annual who's who of the elite gala, she is the envy of even the most sophisticated and wealthy women in attendance. And, if she has to put on some Timberlands and jeans, she doesn't have a problem *thuggin' it out. This woman is the exemplification of style, class, and grace with a touch of naughtiness perfectly mixed. She also loves being the center of attention, and knows how to attract the attention she desires. She is like a mythical Goddess that leaves you in awe.*

This Queen's home is filled with positive energy and peaceful vibes. When you enter, you hear music playing and lots of laughter. Her vast music collection is filled with everything from the oldies but goodies, to the latest jams from all genres. People from all walks and statuses meet at this Queen's home not only to just socialize, but also to find a cure for their blues. For whatever reason they are there, you can bet your bottom dollar that they are being entertained and enjoying themselves to the fullest in a game of tonk, poker, dominoes, spades or bid whist. Of course, the time spent wouldn't be complete without some smack talking. This Queen is so inspiring and the most perfect hostess. Nobody leaves her presence without a hug and a reminder to enjoy this beautiful experience called LIFE.

The Queen of Clubs intuitively understands the importance of living in the moment. To some, it may appear as if she is totally consumed with socializing, club-hopping, and having a good time. However, if you look deeper into what she truly represents, you will come to see that everyone desires to enjoy the pleasures that she has to offer; yours just may be different than hers. She has such a pleasant personality, and she wears her Crown with a smile.

DOWNFALL

If the Queen of Clubs somehow forgets there is more to life than club-hopping, hanging with friends and socializing, her own manifesto—PARTY AND HAVE A GOOD TIME—can also cause her downfall. Fulfilling her need to be at every party and social event because of fear that she is going to miss something can take a toll on her overall well being. Then, there is the REALITY that this Queen is human and has problems and issues to deal with in her own life.

Partying is what she does well, and it is her means of escape, but, seemingly, she cannot come to grips with the fact that all the partying in the world can't make problems disappear; they wait on you.

Seemingly, her need to party is her way of coping with her personal demons, and her advice to others is that which she desires for herself. She tends to stay out until the wee hours of the morning even when she has to rise early to report to her place of employment. When she does, she is often unproductive in the workplace which in turn could—and often does-- threaten her livelihood One can only call in so many times, and miss so many days before one gets a pink-slip or hears, "Your services are no longer needed. Security will escort you OUT."

Unfortunately, she fails to see the damaging consequences of her lifestyle. As a result, she carries a lot of baggage that impedes her from moving forward with her life.

Behind the flirtatious smile and outgoing personality, there is a deep void that a good party just cannot fill. Even though she is fun to be around, she is often the kind of woman most men generally don't take seriously. Although there are exceptions, men look at her for what she displays: a *party girl, someone to have fun with, or a possible one night stand. Truly this Queen has lost sight of the things that should be bringing her the most joy in life when it gets to the point where she would rather be at a party than taking care of priorities like herself, her significant other, or her family.   Although, partying can be her downfall, it can also become her mainstay if she but realizes that she cannot party her problems away (whatever they may be), nor can she always be the life of the party, even though she is definitely the QUEEN OF CLUBS.*

The Queen of Clubs brings love, laughter, positive energy, and good vibes wherever she goes, and the world is in desperate need of Queens like her to show us how to enjoy life. She is truly the life of any party, and without her vigor and ability to make the dullest environment come to life with excitement, some of the people she embraces would be filled with gloom and misery.

KEEP ON CLUBBING QUEEN

AFFIRMATION

OF THE QUEEN OF CLUBS

I Am, the embodiment of the Queen of Clubs. I Am, a joyful expression of the Creator. It is through me that joy and happiness comes into the world. I will embrace my divinity and love myself completely.

I AM the Queen of Clubs!

"*Success is not measured so much by the position that one has reached in life as by the obstacles which he (they) have overcome trying to succeed*"...

Booker T. Washington

3

QUEEN OF DIAMONDS

The Queen of Diamonds is motivated by money and materialism. She has a natural gift when it comes to converting ideas into profits. She is always looking for an opportunity to capitalize off of a potential investment, whether it is minor or major. This woman knows and fully understands the significance of being financially stable, and she knows how to maximize her resources to increase her wealth. She, too, believes in the Golden Rule and the Golden Rule is: "Whoever has the gold (money) makes the rules." Or, at least some of them.

The key to her success is her work ethic. She works extremely hard to get what she needs and wants. While others are partying, lolling around or sleeping, she is thinking, planning and strategizing to achieve her goals.

This Queen is very business-oriented and daring. If she thinks she has the slightest chance of making a profit, she will take the risk. Even when she is taking a risk others may consider totally absurd, there is a 99.9% chance she knows something about the investment or product her competitors do not, because this queen does her homework and takes the necessary precautions to prepare herself before she invests her time, effort, and money into a potentially lucrative venture. Like all successful people she knows that "proper preparation prevents poor performance," and that "those who fail to plan, plan to fail." She understands that knowing is half the battle and execution is the other half.

She understands that the lifespan of a trend or product is one of the determining factors that affect profits. Before she embarks upon a venture, she has intuitively calculated the risk factors—what she stands to profit, what she stands to lose, and what the most effective methods to use to accomplish her goals. She knows it takes money to make money, and although she will invest her own money, she prefers to save it and use other people's money to her advantage.

With her, it is all about having that extra edge, so she stays on top of the game by staying abreast of the latest trends.

In addition to staying alert— keeping her eyes and ears open—her personal business repertoire consists of books, videos and DVDs on subjects like: The Law of Attraction, Positive Affirmations, Money Management, Marketing, Tax Codes and Off Shore Shelters, Real Estate and Commercial Property, Principles of Accounting, Business Communication, Professional Development, Employment Law, and autobiographies of Self-Made Billionaires—to name a few.

Most definitely, The Queen of Diamonds possesses the intellect to be successful in Corporate America, as well as the ability to manifest her innate hustling skills to obtain the finances she needs. This Queen can literally make a dollar out of fifteen-cents. She eats, sleeps, and breathes business. She personifies the saying, "The sky's the limit," and she has absolutely no fear of heights or high stakes.

She takes pride in performing above the expectations that others have set for her, especially those who feel as if their so-called formal education is what makes them successful. She believes in staying prepared because business *opportunities present themselves in some of the strangest places. This Queen is always looking for new opportunities to expand her fortune and if there is a dollar to be made, she wants a percentage of it.*

She understands the importance of networking and staying informed about what's going on with the economy, because major business deals take place every second, every minute, and every hour EVERY DAY.

It is most imperative that she knows who merged with whom, who acquired what, who went public with their stock, who filed bankruptcy; and more importantly, how she can become a part of the next big deal to take place.

This Queen is a money magnet, and she uses her acumen to attract the people who have it or a potentially profitable business on the horizon. Her philosophy is *that people make the world go 'round, but the almighty dollar runs it, and the more one has the more power and influence comes with it.* She is very aware that people are more accommodating when money is involved. She doesn't mind splitting the pie, as long as the cutting is in her favor, so if she has to give a little to make a fortune, so be it. Oh, yes! She is a shrewd business woman.

This Queen is the best at what she does—making money.

Even though it may appear that she is obsessed with making money, this Queen is very compassionate and giving; she extends her knowledge and services to those who inquire of her, and she extends resources and needs for comfort to the less fortunate.

From her style and outer appearance, it is quite obvious that this Queen is high maintenance. She works hard for her money and spends it just as hard because this SHOP-A-HOLIC "shops 'til she drops." Her wardrobe is every fashionista's dream. She dons the latest designs by fashion gurus like K Ramadan, Vonzele Qadir, Gucci, Louis Vitton, Armani, Versace, Yves Saint Laurent, Roberto Cavalli, Vera Wang, Alexander McQueen, Ralph Lauren (Purple and Black Label), Franco Sarto, and Marc Jacobs. But don't get it twisted; this Queen is not above browsing a thrift shop.

Women who frequent being in her presence regards her as a trendsetter. Dressed-up or dressed-down, she has a unique swagger that garners attention. Obviously, this Queen is the "Queen of Fashion" who has mastered the art of looking **Fab-A-Licious**.

Man's best friend may be a dog, but a girl's best friend is for certain a DIAMOND. Who better to showcase this adage than the Queen of Diamonds. Diamonds! Diamonds!! Diamonds!!! This Queen has a plethora in every shape and color that exists. These—and any other gems or precious stones that a woman could possibly desire—can be found in her jewelry box. No doubt, some of her pieces could easily be displayed in the Smithsonian Museum. Her motto is: A Queen can never have too many clothes, too many shoes, or too much money.

This Queen's theme song could very well be The Glamorous Life and her home can be envisioned to rank right up there with those showcased on the show Lifestyle of the Rich and Famous with imported furniture, marble floors, plush Persian rugs, hand-sewn curtains from India, vaulted ceilings, walls adorned with masterpieces, bathrooms resembling world class spas or wellness centers, and a kitchen that rivals that of Five-Star restaurants, vaulted bedrooms with walk-in closets that look like a mini boutique, an entertainment room with all of the amenities to provide guests a memorable time that cannot be rivaled, a garage that shelters an affinity for classic cars and the latest automobiles and SUVs. Perhaps, this is why this Queen has to work so hard for the money. WHEW !!

As you can see, the Queen of Diamonds is a real Go-Getter. Once she sets her mind to making money, trust and believe, she is going to exhaust all of her resources to bring her vision into fruition. She doesn't allow her ideas to remain a moment; she turns them into a lucrative movement. Her Crown is encrusted the jewels of entrepreneurship and piety, and she wears it so well.

DOWNFALL

Because the Queen of Diamonds eats, sleeps and breathes money, her obsession with it could be her downfall if she does not keep focused and keep herself in check. If by chance she abandons her austere work ethics and principles, the lavish lifestyle that she has become accustomed to will surely become a thing of the past. Mismanagement of funds, ill-advised investments, as well as excessive, frivolous spending on shopping-sprees and trips to exotic places should definitely be avoided. Simply because, this queen spends money as if she has an unlimited black card with her name and face on it. Could this, then, be said of her—"A fool and [her] money are soon parted."

The very thought of not having money could easily blind her judgment and cause her to go into a frenzy.   This is when caution is thrown to the wind and uncalculated risks take place that could cost more than she is willing to pay.

Unfortunately, this position is one that can cause the Queen of Diamonds to start using her brilliant mind to devise get-rich-quick schemes. In her unrefined state, she could easily be mistaken for a Gold Digger because in her state of desperation, she will more than likely do whatever is necessary to support her lavish lifestyle and attempt to maintain her image. If the love of money is truly the root of all evil, this Queen is the soil from which it grows.

FORBID that she ever stoops to begging, borrowing, selling her body or more serious crimes just to have the mighty dollars. To allow the money in her bank account to validate her self-worth to the point she will do *anything for it, presents money as her "drug of choice." Truly, she has hit rock bottom on all fronts—mentally, socially, physically and spiritually. Once this Queen forgets SHE IS PRICELESS in the sight of the Creator, it is easy for the enemy of mankind to purchase her worth with the very thing she seemingly loves most. . .MONEY.*

The Queen of Diamonds must always remember that it takes a disciplined yet innovative, mentality to be successful in all of her business endeavors. Although she possesses the potential to make a substantial amount of money, she understands that it takes more than money alone to make a person happy. Karl Marx, a German philosopher and economist, like some others renowned thinkers, contends that there are two types of people on this planet—producers and consumers. The Queen of Diamonds would not support this tenant because she herself is both a producer and a consumer of the finer things in life.

KEEP ON MAKING MONEY QUEEN

AFFIRMATION

OF THE QUEEN OF DIAMONDS

I Am, the embodiment of the Queen of Diamonds. I Am, a prosperous expression of the Creator. It is through me that prosperity comes into the world. I will embrace my divinity and love myself completely.

I AM the Queen of Diamonds

"Wisdom equals knowledge plus courage. You have to not only know what to do and when to do it, but you have to also be brave enough to follow through"...

"J. Kints"

4

THE QUEEN OF SPADES

The Queen of Spades is motivated by knowledge and power. She has a natural gift when it comes to cutting away from the mundane entrapments of the material world. She is very intuitive, and she also possesses impeccable leadership skills. This Queen knows and fully understands the significance of strategizing and executing her plans to the fullest. She believes in the Golden Rule with all of her heart and soul, and the Golden Rule is: Knowledge is power and if used correctly, one can dictate the outcome of any given situation. Her success stems from her ability to use her knowledge, coupled with an indomitable internal fortitude, which enables her to stand strong in the face of adversity.

This Queen is extremely wise and receptive, and she knows that her true power resides within the depths of her spirit. She is well-versed on topics such as, metaphysics, philosophy, religion, history, astrology, botany, ceremonial rituals, and the art of war on every plane of existence. By consulting her inner goddess, she obtains valuable insight that is sure to assist her being successful in all of her undertakings, whatever they may be.

She fully understands the difference between spirituality, religion, belief, and emotionalism. Therefore, she is not easily captivated by soul-stirring sermons, renditions or dialogue filled with sweet empty words of hope and promises. This Queen is a realist, and she deals with life on life's terms and knows all too well that it can be very cruel at times.

Nevertheless, she finds a way to persevere.

With this Queen, every decision is equated to the game of Spades. Her philosophy is: "You have to know how to play the hand you were dealt by the Universal Dealer, because the way you play your cards in life is going to determine the outcome of your situation." How likely is it for anyone to get all of the spades in the hand they have been dealt? Therefore, she pays very close attention to the cards she is dealt before she wastes a valuable card that could ultimately win the game for her. Under no circumstances does she ever make a frivolous cut (decision or move) based on a hunch or emotions because she knows that feelings could impede her from using her Cut-Cards at the appropriate time.

This Queen has been blessed with extraordinary leadership skills. Before she proceeds with any plans or projects, she takes into consideration all of the variables, and calculates any potential casualties that may be encountered. At the same time, she does not believe in thwarting opportunities, as it is rare that the same opportunity is presented twice. Therefore, she prepares herself thoroughly and executes her plans with precision.

When it comes to love, business, or war, she weighs the pros and cons before making a commitment. But, once she does, she is prepared for the challenge and is in it for the long haul. Her methods of operation consist of three components: Devise a Sound Plan, Obtain Proper Resources, and Being Swift and Proficient.

No challenge is too great for this Queen. She is a true master when it comes to absorbing knowledge and being able to use it for a noble purpose or to her advantage at war.

This Queen's ability to enter your spirit completely undetected is one of the skills that make her so mysterious and dangerously effective. She possesses the power to disarm the most alert and suspicious individuals, causing them to submit to her every beckon, or—at worse—beg for her mercy if or when she has to swing her sword and come out fighting if the situation calls for such drastic measures.

This Queen is a true occultist at heart, for she is highly intrigued with the deeper meaning of life, she is one who relies on specific rather than general knowledge about a subject.

Unlike the masses, she is not afraid to question the myths and fables that have been passed down from generation to generation as the absolute truth, by those who profit from the ignorance of the misinformed. This Queen abhors ignorance, and she refuses to allow the traditional mindset of a male dominated society impede her from knowing the mysteries of the universe. She is the Queen that other women secretly admire, because she is courageous enough to partake of the so-called forbidden fruit (Knowledge) that makes one all knowing like the gods. In fact, she is the living manifestation presented in many of the great classical literary works (*i.e.,* *The Book of Coming Forth By Day,* *The Art of War,* *The Book of Five Rings,* *The I Ching,* *The Prince (Machiavelli),* *The 48 Laws of Power,* *and The Art of Seduction*) perfectly mixed with a thorough knowledge of the ideals presented in *The Holy Bible,* *The Quran,* *The Metu Neter Oracle System,* *Yoruba,* *Santeria,* *Supreme Wisdom,* *The Kabala,* *Yoga,* *Qi Gong,* and the *Secrets of the Sacred Goddess.*

As the Queen of the Spades, she has a dualistic nature. She is definitely in tune with this aspect of herself that entails the ability to ascend to higher *levels of spiritual enlightenment and the power to activate the inner-strength to cut away from negative situations that may pose a threat to her well-being. She also pays close attention to her dreams for they are her connection to the various realms of existence and provide her with divine insight.*

She is a practitioner of sciences that the ill-informed and society has labeled as sorcery, witchcraft, voodoo, as well as other inaccurate names for the knowledge she possess. For her, the universe is a reservoir of resources waiting to be used to invoke the infinite powers of her spirit. Being well aware of the reciprocal nature of energy, she also projects hers with the utmost discipline and mastery.

This Queen is among those persons who seek knowledge for themselves, and in so doing, she is adamantly opposed to being told what should or should not be adhered to or believed. Through studying, meditating, research, and sitting at the feet of Elders, she has come to the realization that the secrets of the universe has always been in that beautiful mind of hers. However, if this Queen has to don a suit of armor, the warrior within her will rise to the occasion and provide her with the necessary weapons to slay her enemies both externally and internally. This Queen is the sage and the sorcerer with a heart that can be warm and gentle, or cold as ice. In war, she takes no prisoners.

Having the privilege of entering her home, one is greeted with adornments of esoteric symbolism and embraced by an ancient community that has perfected the science of spiritual mastery. Although the atmosphere is mysterious, it arouses curiosity and lends to the feeling of being a traveler stepping into a time machine with sole control of the destination and the experiences to be encountered. Rooms are designated for meditation, yoga, research, study groups, spiritual cleansings, and destiny readings.

The warrior nature in this queen is satisfied by her affinity for weaponry. Her arsenal may include magnificent swords; beautifully embellished guns, cross bows, daggers, spears and shields; and rare ancient collectible artifacts dealing with war and survival. Her home is her private sanctuary where she prepares herself for spiritual and earthly encounters of peace or war in the arenas of life whether personal or business.

The Queen of Spades is a true markswoman, always focused and weighing her options before she takes action. This Queen is wise enough to know when to seek counsel, and courageous enough to execute without fear of any potential repercussions. It is better to have her on your side than against you, because as the old adage goes, "It's all fair in love and war," and she is skillfully dangerous. She wears her Crown with authority and confidence.

DOWNFALL

If the Queen of Spades gets consumed chasing the mundane entrapments of the material world, instead of being a fierce leader that she's known to be, she becomes a blind follower. Therefore, she forfeits her power by not applying her intuition, knowledge, and leadership skills which are the keys to her success. Also, mistaking information for knowledge will be a major cause of failure, because this Queen's strengths lie in knowing, planning, and executing. When she doesn't plan her undertakings, although she very knowledgeable and proficient, things tend to blow up in her face, and she abhors being embarrassed. So, it is imperative for this Queen to keep a full-proof plan.

If this Queen is opposed or feel threatened in the slightest manner, she can become very aggressive, domineering, and manipulative. Her temper can go from ice cold to burning hot with one word, which means she will either freeze you or burn you with her looks, words, and actions. Her tongue is the fierce combination of a sharp sword and a burning flame, and when she's angry you never know what will come out of her mouth or what she will do.

If out of desperation she uses her Cut-Cards (decision making skills) in a frivolous and reckless manner, her life becomes extremely chaotic due to the lack of order, balance, and harmony. When she loses control, seek refuge because all hell is about to break loose.

When this Queen stops questioning and starts accepting things on face value, the characteristics that she is admired for becomes her greatest weakness. She is known for giving sound advice; however, she must also apply the same advice that she readily gives to others.

This Queen should always monitor her temper, her tongue, her need to always be in command, and how she communicates with people. If she doesn't, her aggressive demeanor is going to land her in disagreements, arguments, and worse, war. And once this Queen has lost control, her life will take a downward spiral, and unlike the proverbial phoenix, it is rare that she rises from the ashes without any scars, if she rises at all. The sword swings both ways, and if she is not careful she will become a victim of her own hands, and ultimately self-destruct.

The great Sun Tzu profoundly stated in The Art of War *that "being unconquerable lies within yourself. Being conquerable lies within your enemy." Ignorance of one's self has always been, and will always be the true enemy. Therefore, the Queen of Spades must always remember to keep her weapons (mind and tongue) sharp, loaded, and ready for war against ignorance—her sworn eternal enemy.*

Indeed, the Queen of Spades is the protector and teacher of the sacred sciences and, because of her courage; she inspires others who were once afraid to diligently seek knowledge. She knows the truth will set one free, only when they are fearless enough to challenge the lies that have them in bondage. Nevertheless, if she is not careful, she can become a victim of her own weapons and ultimately self-destruct. However, this Queen is extremely meticulous, keeps a full proof plan, is always prepared, and ready for the many challenges life brings her way.

KEEP ON FIGHTING QUEEN

AFFIRMATION

OF THE QUEEN OF SPADES

I Am, the embodiment of the Queen of Spades. I Am, a wise expression of the Creator. It is through me that justice comes into the world. I will embrace my divinity and love myself completely.

I AM the Queen of Spades!

"We can't change our past, but our future is spotless, and it would behoove us to do something extraordinary with it."

R. Brown

5

THE TRANSFORMATION

This is where your NEW LIFE begins. If you truly believe in the power of forgiveness and redemption, the first step to moving forward with your NEW LIFE is to forgive yourself for any bad decision you made in the past that still haunts you. Erykah Badu has a song called "Bag Lady," and in the song she sings about women carrying baggage that is weighing them down spiritually, mentally, emotionally, as well as physically. Unfortunately, carrying old baggage impedes us from living in the NOW. Do yourself a big favor and leave your past where it's at, in the past.

Next, it's time to redeem yourself and restore your integrity, your high moral standards, and your impeccable character. It's of utmost importance to understand that one's integrity, high moral standards, and impeccable character has nothing to do with one's social status. Titles doesn't define the person, the person defines the title by how they treat others.

Queen, this is your opportunity to construct the blueprint for your NEW LIFE. Consider this, among all of the creatures that were created, humans were given the WILL-POWER to choose the course of their lives. Whether you have been properly informed or not, YOU alone, decide how your personal journey will ultimately become. From this point on, everything you thought you were must be reanalyzed. Some of us have held on to what we were taught about ourselves as children, regardless of how out of line with our values those beliefs may be. For some reason or another they are still being held on to, let them go.

Today, Free yourself from the ball and chain (negative thoughts and beliefs) that have you in bondage. It takes courage to move forward with your life; however, the commitment to breaking free is worth the rewards. You may be familiar with the infamous snake headed lady Medusa, and looking into her face would turn you into stone. It has been said if we don't face our fears, they will always be in our face. However, when you are courageous enough to say to yourself with conviction:

(Psalms 23) 1. The Lord (God Conscious-Indwelling Intelligence) is my shepherd (Guide); I shall not want (Be devoid of resources). 2. He maketh me lie down in green pastures (Rest in a safe dwelling): He leadeth me beside still waters (Peace and refreshment). 3. He restoreth my soul (Heal me internally); He leadeth me in the paths of righteousness (Moral conduct) for his names sake. 4. Yea, though I walk through the valley (Life, trials and tribulations) of the shadow of death, I will fear no evil (Challenges, hurt, harm or danger): for though art with me; thy rod (Knowledge, power, and authority) and thy staff (Love,

wisdom, and protection) they comfort me (Put my mind at ease). 5. Thou prepares a table before me in the presence of mine enemies (Makes me Prosperous); thou anointest my head with oil (Consecrates my head with knowledge); my cup runneth over (Life filled with abundance). 6. Surely goodness and mercy shall follow me all the days of my life; and I will dwell in the house of the Lord forever (Blessings, Security, and Eternity). When you know who you are (Your True Self), not the persona you identify with, as well as whose you are (Understand your Essesnce), you can walk through any valley knowing the victory is yours. Claim it!!

It is great to have assistance on our journey; however, there comes a time when we have to take our destiny into our own hands. I am more than certain, there is a part of you that longs to tap into your hidden talents and gifts, with aspirations to unwrap them in a manner that will allow you to manifest your greatness. As the old saying goes: "There is no time like the present."

(The Powers of Your Crown)

The Queen of Hearts, showed you how to love and let your presence be a present to others...

The Queen of Clubs, showed you how to enjoy yourself and the many pleasures that life has to offer...

The Queen of Diamonds, showed you how to provide for yourself and handle your finances...

The Queen of Spades, showed you how to free your mind and defend yourself on every plane of existence ...

Now, this is where your personal journey begins; be courageous and see life through new eyes and consolidate the Powers of Your Crown...

6

BECOMING

THE COMPLETE QUEEN

Although the reader has been formally introduced to four Queens, in reality, the traits and characteristics of each are the spiritual, mental, emotional, and physical make-up of One Beautiful Woman. Simply put, every woman is a combination of all four queens. Think about that for a minute.

Perhaps, that was unbelievable leading one to question whether all of this really make up the character of ONE woman. Certainly, the women who read this went "Hmmmm, really now." Men on the other hand probably shook their heads and scanned the room for the nearest exit should he have to escape. In actuality, men, these Queens are just waiting for you to discover them and appreciate and respect them for what they have to offer you.

As the author, my response to the reader is, YES! I, and a number of men have dialogued with, have at some time or another personally met at least two or more of these Queens in one or more of our female associates in whatever role they were playing in our lives at the time.

Women, these Queens are just waiting on you to awaken and recognize ALL OF WHOM YOU REALLY ARE and to become the BEST COMPLETE WOMAN YOU CAN BECOME.

Your affirmation should very well be:

"I AM" a combination of all four queens and regardless of my spiritual, mental, emotional, and/or physical state. . . . . . . "I AM !"

Once women begin to seriously internalize this TRUTH about themselves, it could prove to be a tremendously advantageous benefit to sift through all of the traits and consciously accept and develop all of the ones they would like to edify; to show themselves as a woman distinctively different—yet alike in some ways—from every other woman they encounter in the whole wide world. After all, there are billions of women on this planet, but there is only one YOU.

When you consciously choose to totally embrace everything positive about yourself—from the outer physical appearance, to the inner soul and all that it governs; to the spirit which encourages you to partake of all the good that our Creator has provided; and everything in between that lends itself to taking the necessary measures to develop a nurturing, loving, positive self-image should be something that every woman would want to do.

You are probably saying I just read that somewhere in this book. You did! It's in here TWICE (see Preface) to re-enforce the significance *of accepting everything that makes you the unique Complete Queen that you strive to be through your words, actions, and deeds. The beauty about striving to become a Complete Queen is that women can be empowered by the queens in this book to continue to be the strong, beautiful women that they are, and to change the things they don't like about themselves or some of the directions their lives are headed.*

Know and understand that women are Divinity personified. Once they begin to embrace their Divinity wholeheartedly, life will take on a totally new meaning and become more fulfilling.

Women have always been *phenomenal, extraordinary, and absolutely amazing*, and those who have already consciously realized that they are the embodiment of the author Dr. Maya Angelou's *Phenomenal Woman*, probably already have the courage and confidence needed to embrace this new—yet old—way of viewing women.

A thorough understanding of how and when to apply the principles of each Queen will assist in finding a personal balance point. Will the traits and characteristics of all Four Queens be mastered over night? Of course not. This level of Queenhood takes time and incorporates an inventory and self- study, learning from personal experiences, not being afraid to question what is in variance to intuition, studying the lives of women who made a significant difference in society, dialoguing with other Queens who fought to rise above traditional conditioning; and, most importantly, acknowledging personal strengths and being brutally honest about any weaknesses.

There is a metamorphosis that must take place in order for this level of spiritual, mental, emotional, and *physical transformation to take place. Sorry, there are no magic wands. As with all things worth having in life, there has to be some kind of sacrifice to remind us what we gave up to get where we're at. I know it can be extremely hard giving up some things you have conditioned yourself to believe that you just can't live without. Well, in order for the Truth about your Divine Self to set you free, you must know the lie(s) that have you in bondage. On the doorway of the Great Pyramid of Khufu it states: "Know Thyself." How much do you really Know about your Divine Self? Freedom comes with a Price.*

"Sometimes you've got to let everything go—purge yourself...If you are unhappy with anything...whatever it is bringing you down get rid of it. Because you'll find that when you're free, your true creativity, your true self comes out."

Tina Turner

7

REPROGRAMMING

YOUR SPIRIT

It's been said that humans are spiritual beings taking on an earthly experience. If so, then it is imperative that both the body and spirit are healthy and vibrant in order to manifest the traits and characteristics of each Queen. The spirit is the essence of who we are, and it should ultimately shape the course of our lives.

Positive energy and imagery invigorates the spirit. Contrarily, negative energy and imagery devitalizes it and causes us to feel drained and disoriented. Regardless of what challenges life presents, we determine the health of our spirit. A healthy spirit leads to a healthy life. **What are you feeding yours?**

That being said, it is necessary to have a working knowledge of how the spiritual anatomy functions. Every spirit has an anatomy, and unlike the physical body, the spiritual anatomy is invisible to the carnal eye. To access it one has to withdraw from the material world and go within in order to awaken the dormant faculties that connects us to the creative force that permeates the entire universe.

Through my research I have found that all cultures have a Creation Story, which clearly states that we are made in the Image and Likeness of The Creator. Unfortunately, this Image and Likeness is often given a physical corpus, which intern, distorts the inner meaning of this simple, yet complex analogy of the spirit. The Spirit is the animating force of our existence. Some call the Spirit

(Energy, Qi, Chi, Holy Ghost, Life Force and other names). The name you are most comfortable using will be suffice.

Dr. Ra Un Nefer Amen gives an eloquent breakdown of the The Kamtic Tree of Life (Paut Neteru) and how it correlates to our Spiritual Anatomy. Please pay very close attention to how we have always used these principles, but unfortunately, they were not properly introduced to us. Learning this system will change your life instantaneously.

Dr. Ra Un Nefer Amen states each sphere represents a different quality of the Spirit.

Kamitic Tree of Life

The Paut Neteru(Spiritual Faculties)

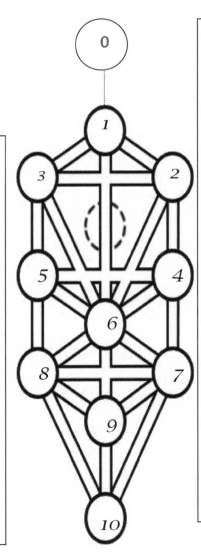

0. Amen/Oludamare
Source of life and
Inner Peace

1. Ausar/Obatala
Omnipresence True
Self   Unity with ALL
Indwelling
Intelligence

2. Tehuti/Orunmila
Omniscience, Divine
Will Communicated
to man/woman.
Intuition

3. Sekert/Babaluaye
Omnipotence
Spiritual Power,
Divine Plan/ Destiny

4. Maat /Aje Chigulia
Divine Law
Interdependence
between God and
Man/Woman

5. HeruKhuti/Ogun
Divine Justice
Law of Karma

6. Heru /Shango
Will Power
Freedom of Choice

7.Het-Heru/Oshun
Imagination Ability
to Visualize, The seat
of Joy

8. Sebek/Eshu
Power of Thoughts,
Words, The Intellect

9. Auset/Yemeya
 Power of
Transcendence,
Receptivity,
Nurturing

10. Geb/Ernile
 Life Force,
Vitality, Earthly
resources

If you analyze the Tree of Life you will notice every sphere is connected to each other, which implies there is an interdependence at work within our Spiritual Anatomy. Peace is the natural state of our spirit, and when we identify with our True Self beyond our personality, it puts us in a position to benefit from the other spheres. Ponder on this for a moment, you have access to (2) Intuition, (3) Spiritual power, (4) Divine order, (5) Divine justice and protection, (6) Will-power and freedom to choose, (7) Creativity and joy, (8) Power think to and affirm, (9) The ability to transcend traditional conditioning, and (10) Access to material resources that will improve the quality of your living standards. However, you must internalize this knowledge and become one with it to receive the greatest benefits.

By no means am I suggesting you forget everything you have learned thus far. However, I am strongly suggesting that you re-evaluate everything you have been taught about yourself from a spiritual standpoint. Being that healing starts in the spirit, wouldn't it make perfect sense to develop your very own personal Spiritual Curriculum? When it comes to our personal well-being, unfortunately, there's no one size fits all solution. But out of grace and mercy, we have been blessed with the "Keys to the Kingdom."

All of the great souls—wise women and men—conclude that *the Creator is an all pervasive spirit, and in order to worship the Creator, we must do it in spirit and truth*, not out of spirit and lies. Truth transforms lives while lies promote denial. Imagine having access to that kind of power when dealing with life's many trials. Well, we as Divine beings have that power. *Oh!* If only we would just stop imagining and start tapping into it.

Once again, it takes courage to look into the mirror of your soul, but when you do, you will find Spiritual treasures that are priceless. Trust me; they are waiting to be discovered.

"If you can control the diameter of a person's thoughts, without a doubt, you will surely control the circumference of their actions."

Minister L. Farakhan

8

REPROGRAMMING

YOUR MIND

Just as the spirit is the essence of our being, think of the mind as a garden, and the seeds planted in it will ultimately shape life's reality. The saying, "You reap what you sow." should always make us conscious of the seeds we sow into our brilliant minds. Some sages teach their students that it's just mind over matter. The truth is, what's on the mind really does matter when it comes to improving the quality of life.

The mental (mind) state is comprised of thoughts, beliefs, feelings, and attitudes. Understanding how each one of these components contributes to decision making individually as well as collectively will assist greatly on the journey to becoming a Complete Queen.

The mind is like a huge magnet. Thoughts that are constantly dwelled on will eventually attract a corresponding experience in some area of life. Even those thoughts that are buried at the subconscious level will eventually give life to something positive or negative in due time. So once again, be cognizant of the fact that seeds planted and nurtured in the garden of the mind have more power than one may realize. In this case, *as a woman thinketh, so she strives to become.*

"When one learns they are in total control of their feelings and emotions, they come to the realization that what others say and do only have the power they allow them to have. Why give someone or some thing what's always been yours?"

Maa-Kheru

9

UNDERSTANDING FEELINGS AND EMOTIONS

Most people suffer from Cognitive Emotional Dissonance (CED). This means that thoughts and feelings aren't in harmony with each other. However, becoming the Complete Queen necessitates working diligently at living a life filled with love, order, balance, and harmony.

Feelings are synonymous to emotions. Emotions can be broken down into two words: Energy and Motion. Energy is a force or power. Motion implies some form of movement or animation. The stimuli for feelings is based on thoughts and beliefs, and once this energy is put into motion, in-sperience (a coined word) is set into motion. Unlike "experience," "in-sperience" is the process of dealing with situations internally with the mind or psyche rather than those experienced outside of the body.

Feelings derive from what is thought, believed, experienced, or seen in a situation or in a person. When something is perceived as pleasurable, it creates a sense of joy, contentment, and happiness. However, when the perception is negative and not in alignment with core values, it causes feelings of anger, disappointment, frustration, and ultimately sadness. This gives credence to the saying "Perception is Reality," and the way a person or situation is perceived determines whether the response will be positive or negative.

Let's do a quick exercise. Think about something that brings pleasure and makes you FEEL good about yourself. Hold that image in the mind for a few seconds. Do you feel the energy in motion? How did it make you feel? Were you in control of your feelings? If, not, then do the exercise again and remember that you can always control how you feel. When you allow circumstances and other people to make you feel a certain way about anything, you relinquish your power to consciously control how you want to feel about it.

Remember, your feelings are based on your thoughts and beliefs. It has been said that feelings and emotions are good servants, but they make poor masters. This is not to say that feelings should not be expressed for they are necessary components of the *spiritual and emotional make-up that makes us human. However, they must be closely monitored. Just because you may feel a certain way or feel like doing something, doesn't justify actually acting upon those feelings. To do so or to allow them to roam freely could lead to detrimental consequences. You've heard the old saying: "Trouble is easy to get in, but hard to get out of."*

"I've learned that people will forget what you said, people will forget what you did, but people will never forget how you made them feel"...

Dr. Maya Angelou

10

DEVELOPING

A POSITIVE ATTITUDE

Attitude is an EXPRESSION of thoughts, beliefs, and feelings. There are great benefits that come with having a positive attitude, and there are great detriments that come with having a negative attitude. There is a saying that "attitude equals altitude." If so, then it is important to understand that your attitude about life will determine the heights you are capable of ascending to, as well as the lowly depths to which you can descend. Therefore, a choice has to be made, because no two things can occupy the same space at the same time.

Expressing a Positive Attitude involves such abstracts as being honest, loving, joyful, caring, objective, open minded, patient, hopeful, understanding, kind, peaceful, forgiving, responsible, firm, just, humility and gratitude. Once these positives are firmly planted in the soil of the mind, a noticeable outward change in behavior will reflect the inward change, which in turn will influence how people respond to you. A Positive Attitude can help to keep things in perspective even when it seems that life is falling apart.

Yes, there might be times when trying to exemplify a positive attitude will surely become a serious struggle. Acknowledge the struggle. To do so is a sign of inner growth. Recognizing that something is not right is the first step to challenging the Negative Attitude that wants to take center stage. Again, remember that you are in control of the attitude you choose to express at any given moment. As a reminder, sometimes it's good to do an Attitude check.

Let's face it; no one is exempt from having one of those days when it seems as if everything in the world is going wrong. The job, the kids, your mate, even the smallest things that you usually ignore have you at that tipping point. You've been there before, right?

Well, can you imagine what was on mother Mary's mind when King Herod wanted her son dead? Being that women will do whatever's necessary to save their children, is it possible that sweet Mother Mary had some thoughts that only her and the Creator know about? However, even with that kind of pressure, she never lost her positive attitude because she knew the Creator would provide her with the peace that she sought. The moral of the story is, Mother Mary showed us that a cool head always prevails.

As a reminder, "Your life is determined not so much by what life brings to you as by the attitude you bring to life; not so much to you as by the way your mind looks at what happens."

(Khalil Gibran)

1 Corinthians 3: 16-17 (KJV)

"16. Know ye not that ye are the temple of God, and that the Spirit of God dwelleth in you. 17. If any man/woman defile the temple of God, him/her shall God destroy; for the temple of God is Holy, which temple ye are?" What a Question...

11

YOUR BODY — YOUR TEMPLE

Your spirit can be healthy. Your mind can be sharp. Your emotions and feelings can be balanced. Your attitude can be positive. Your communication skills can be superb. But, if your Body is not a fit vehicle for the Creator to work through, it will be extremely difficult to achieve your purpose for existing.

Your Body is symbolic of a Sacred Temple, has many similarities to the planet earth, and should never be defiled. Women have been given one of the greatest missions by the Creator. What's that, you may be asking? Bringing Life into the world.

Churches, mosque, cathedrals, and state of the art buildings that cost millions of dollars are like worthless rags compared to the Body. The Body is the SACRED TEMPLE.

Man built all of the lifeless edifices he calls sacred and holy. The Creator created and gave life to the Body—The SACRED TEMPLE in which the Holy

Spirit dwells. **Who then is the better architect and designer?**

Since the Body is the temple, it is important to treat it with the utmost respect by providing it with the best possible nourishment. Just because the food looks good and smells good does not mean it is good for the Body, and praying over a plate of food does not make it healthy.

The composition and physical make-up of every Body is different and what may benefit or affect one may not benefit or affect another. Commune with the Body and learn what foods provide it with what it needs without adverse reactions.

In order to keep the Body healthy, not only do we have to watch what we eat, we also have to exercise it. Of course, every woman does not aspire to be a female body builder, but every woman should desire to be physically fit. Walking, jogging, yoga, qi gong, swimming, hiking, and other activities not only burn calories for the weight conscious woman, they also provide great benefits for good health.

Everyone has an ideal self-image, and there's nothing wrong with that. However, there comes a time when we must take inventory of what we're putting in our bodies if we want to keep our Temple Holy. Some may say it's not what you put in it but what comes out of it. I say, tell that to a person who has diabetes, high blood pressure, acid reflux, and the many diseases that plagues our Body. Sure, we can eat whatever we like, treat our Body like worthless rags, but know for a surety your Body will treat you the way you treat it.

"Good communicators know how to speak, what to speak, where to speak, to whom to speak, but most importantly, when to be absolutely silent"...

The meaning of silence

12

COMMUNICATION SKILLS

People generally form opinions of others within the first 10 seconds of being in their presence; consequently, communication skills are ultimately the determining factor in how one is perceived by others. The tongue is one of the smallest organs in the body, but not too many people know how to master it. Simply put, this small organ can cause some big problems in life if one doesn't know how to control or use it wisely.

In addition to speaking, another first impression can be delivered by the way one listens to others. Being a great active listener is an invaluable communication skill. Active listening is being able to summarize what someone says and repeat it back with a constructive response or question. Of course, you have the freedom to respond any way you choose, however, the ultimate goal is to create a comfort zone for the people with whom you may find yourself communicating with.

It could be an advantage to know the four most common styles of communication (Passive, Aggressive, Passive-Aggressive and Assertive). Passive communicators do not express their feelings when challenged by others. Aggressive communicators often use strong language that has a tendency to offend others. Passive-Aggressive communicators express negative feelings in an aggressive, unassertive passive way. The goal is to always be an assertive communicator, saying what you need to say in a confident, intelligible, and respectful manner. This knowledge could very well come in handy when trying to make an impression or just simply to be a good communicator in general.

In addition to oral (*both language usage and speaking*) and listening skills, people do not just pay attention to what is said; they also observe body language and read facial expressions. They also tend to listen to word choices, so striving broadening one's vocabulary would be wise. After all, it is not always what you say, but how you say it.

As you become the Complete Queen, you will understand the significance of being an effective communicator. Just think about the many roles you play in the lives of your love ones and associates, as well as how you communicate with each one of them. Now, that takes a skill that can't be bought, you have to learn it on the job. Learn to listen with your heart, and respond with words filled with love, wisdom compassion, and encouragement.

"When we learn how to unify our spirit, mind, heart and feelings, we begin to awaken a force that gives us the power to change the world"...

Ausar Amen-Ra

13

CHARACTERISTICS

OF THE FOUR QUEENS

The Queen of Hearts represents the loving, nurturing, maternal, humble, healing, feminine, security minded, accommodating, sweet mannered, comfort loving, compassionate, friendly, benevolent, receptive, emotional, appeasing, mild mannered, *fertile, domestic, relaxed, and dedicated aspect of a woman.*

The Queen of Clubs *represents the social, joyous, pleasure seeking, seductive, attractive, graceful, imaginative, creative, amorous, attention loving, merry, entertaining, loving to travel, great dancing, charming, lascivious, sensual, and full of excitement aspect of a woman.*

The Queen of Diamonds *represents the business minded, tactful, optimistic, analytical, competitive, extravagant, savvy, materialistic, independent, courageous, financially successful, thrifty, risk taking, entrepreneurial, energetic, grandiose,* generous, charitable, observant, ambitious, executive, the need for financial stability aspect of a woman.

The Queen of Spades represents the knowledgeable, just, liberal, tenacious, aggressive, intuitive, impartial, self-aware, disciplined, organized, patient, hard working, abstract, visual thinking, law abiding, honest, insightful and circumspect, culturally inclined, and warrior aspect of a woman.

Every Woman is born a Queen, but not Every Woman will acknowledge herself as such. She, and she alone, will determine how she carries herself on this tumultuous journey called life. She is the Master and the slave, picking and choosing when to be a teacher, and when she will allow herself to be taught. Nevertheless, she's always in control of her fate...

Maa-Kheru

14

MASTERING YOUR FOUR QUEENS
UP CLOSE AND PERSONAL WITH THE AUTHOR

As with all things in life, each Queen has negative traits and characteristics that must certainly be transcended. Of course you know yourself better than anyone else, and I'm quite sure you know which traits and characteristics you need to say goodbye to. Trust me; there is a gift in saying **Goodbye!** to old behavior patterns and habits that impede you from moving forward with your life.

There comes a time when you must examine your old way of thinking and make a paradigm shift that is in harmony with how you want to live your life.

I chose to focus more on the positive traits of each Queen. However, it was necessary to bring to your sphere of awareness that each Queen also has her downfalls. Once again, becoming the Complete Queen requires you to examine every aspect of your life—the good, the bad and the ugly—and to maintain a sense of who you are at the same time.

Now that you have a thorough understanding of the traits and characteristics that each Queen possesses, more than likely you have found a Queen that you identify with more than the others. Once again for clarity, every woman who reads this book needs to understand, and always keep in mind that she IS a combination of all four Queens. Even if you cannot wrap your mind around these ideals right now, these traits and characteristics have always been an essential component of your spiritual, mental, emotional, and physical make-up and they can be awakened.

As I stated before, becoming the Complete Queen will not happen overnight. I am sorry; it just doesn't work like that! If that were the case, there would not be a need for a book like this. However, as you study and implement these principles into your life on a daily basis, you will insperience a transformation that cannot be explained in words alone. Of course there is plenty of work to be done, but the benefits of striving to become the Complete Queen will immediately add value to your life.

As you strive to become the Complete Queen there has to be a spirit, mind, and body integration. All of your faculties must work together for one common cause, regardless of the undertaking. You must learn the Queens. You must live the Queens. You must be the Queens. You must become the embodiment of All Four Queens, which gives you access to their secrets and powers.

Being that each Queen has special qualities of her own; there will be times when invoking the personality traits of a specific Queen may be more appropriate due to the nature of the situation. With each Queen comes a different temperament, and the way you approach a challenge will always dictate the outcome. You can either use the passion of the Queen of Hearts, take the nonsensical route of the Queen of Clubs, be shrewd and calculating like the Queen of Diamonds, or take the serious, sometimes aggressive approach of the Queen of Spades. When in doubt ask yourself, *What would the Complete Queen do?*

Studying the mythos of Ancient Kush, Egypt, India, Nigeria, Israel, Greece, Rome, and various cultures around the world will expand your understanding of how each Queen was exemplified. You may be familiar with the names of Goddesses and other great women such as: Auset, Isis, Yemeya, Mary—the mother of Jesus, Het-Heru, Hathor, Oshun, Lakshmi, Venus, Mary Magdalene, Ma'at, Tara, Gaia, Oya, Maat, Laksmi, Mama Freda, Diana, Athena, Padmini , Mama Wata, and Neb-Het just to name a few.

However, a deeper study of these mythos and characteristics of what each goddess or woman represents will bring you face to face with the Queen in the mirror. The ancients used nature, songs, signs and symbols to tell stories of what was termed as the Sacred Feminine, and by now, you should be courageous enough to awaken the Queen that resides within the depths of your being. Everything starts with a vision, so visualize yourself becoming the Complete Queen, endowed with spiritual gifts that will provide you with insight and resources you will need to utilize in any situation life brings your way.

Mastering the traits and characteristics of the Four Queens will honestly take some hard work; however, reading this book has embarked you on a journey that will take you one step closer to evolving into the Complete Queen you were *created to be. Your commitment is the key to being successful, and I cannot imagine what can be more important to you than becoming the BEST YOU.*

You were made in the image and likeness of our Creator and placed in the most beautiful feminine form. It IS YOU who brings life into this world; it is THROUGH YOU the world experiences the loving, fun, business-oriented, omniscient existence of the Creator.

Regardless of which Queen you personally indentify with, always remember, YOU are a combination of all four Queens. Master them, and you Master yourself. Now that you have been informed about your potential and capabilities, put on your Crown, and wear it with dignity, pride and honor, as you strive to become the Complete Queen.

(Final words from the Author)

I sincerely pray that my words will inspire you to strive to be the absolute best that you can possibly be. I'm quite sure there are some things that made you look at yourself in a totally different manner, as well as say, this queen is just like my mother, grandmother, auntie, sister, cousin, friend, or someone that you know. Of course there are so many things to say about a topic this extensive; however, it is my intention to spark some much needed dialogue between women and men. Hopefully you enjoyed yourself.

Peace and Blessings...

Bibliograpy

Sited Works

The Metu Neter Series (Ra Un Nefer Amen)

The Handbook of Yoruba Religious Concepts (Baba Ifa Karade)

Gemstones (Alisha Byrd)

As a man thinketh (James Allen)

Chief Yu-Ya Assan Anu (Enlightenment and Transformation-Blogtalkradio)

The Holy Bible (NIV)

Conversations with Real Women

ABOUT THE AUTHOR

Alex Clark (Ausar Amen-Ra) is a native of North Carolina. He is a motivational speaker, community activist, youth advocate, and entrepreneur. Alex is a modern day renaissance man with an old soul, and he's on a mission to inspire others to see the greatness that resides within themselves through writing thought provoking books and public speaking. He believes that everyone has a purpose, and once they find it, they will make a significant difference in the world, or at least in someone's life. His mantra is "Let your Presence be a Present to others."

Contact us @

thecompletequeen@gmail.com